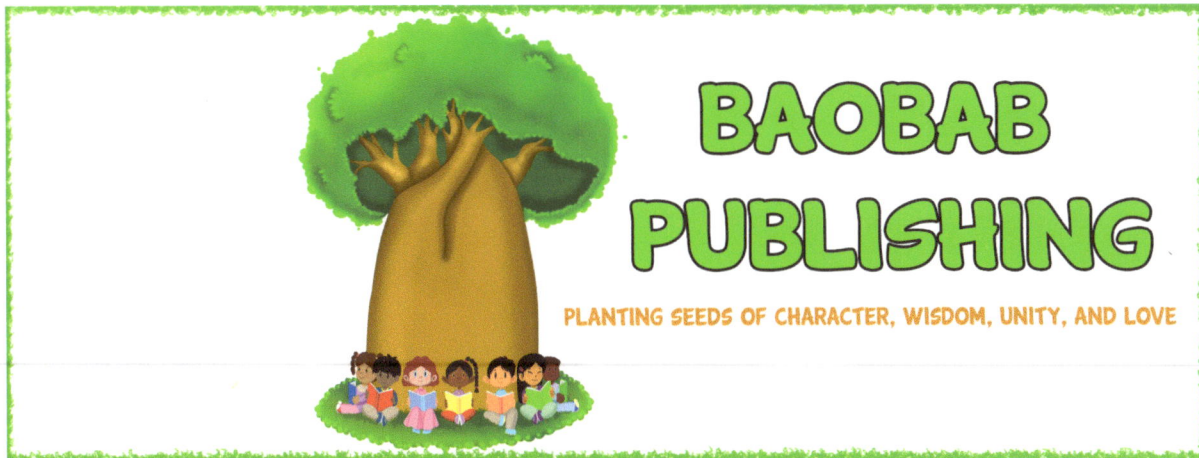

BAOBAB PUBLISHING

PLANTING SEEDS OF CHARACTER, WISDOM, UNITY, AND LOVE

Text and Illustrations Copyright © 2016 by
Schertevear Q. Watkins and Essence Watkins
Address all inquiries to:
Baobab Books
Email: bbfbooks@gmail.com

ISBN-13:
978-0998223148 (Baobab Publishing)

ISBN-10:
099822314X

"Yuk!" Rylan complained as he glanced at his cabbage rolls. "I hate cabbage."

"You need to eat at least half of it," Mom insisted.

"Mine tastes yummy," Abigail said smacking on a mouth full of cabbage covered in ketchup.

Rylan pretended he didn't hear Mom
say to eat half of his cabbage.
Instead, he began gobbling down his
meatloaf and macaroni and cheese.
"Are you not eating your cabbage like
Mom asked you to?" Dad asked Rylan.

Rylan chugged down a mouthful of cabbage and pretended it was making him puke. "Well, since you're so sick, I suggest you go on to bed!" demanded Dad.

Rylan went to his room, and began reading a comic book. Skylar walked in, "Ooh, I'm going to tell Dad that you're not sick." "I don't care," Rylan replied. "I'm still never eating vegetables, no matter what."

The next day in the cafeteria,
Rylan ate his sandwich, minus the
lettuce, and tomatoes. He then
gobbled down his orange slices.
The green beans went untouched.

Everyone else was eating the stuff he didn't and were telling Rylan how good it was. "I don't care." Rylan replied. "I'm still never eating vegetables, no matter what."

All week, Rylan got sent to his room early for trying to make himself barf up his vegetables at dinner. One night during dinner, Mom compared broccoli to trees just cut down and stacked in a pile to be ground.

Saturday the family went bowling. After playing a few games they ate lunch. Rylan enjoyed the sweet potato pudding so much that he asked Dad for more. "Do you realize you just ate a potato?" Skylar asked. "I thought you hated vegetables?" "I do!" Rylan affirmed.

When the family got back home, Rylan ran to his room, angry. He said that he'd been tricked into eating potatoes. "I bet he ate all of his vegetables to get those muscles," Mom said, referring to the wrestling man Rylan was holding in his hand. "Do vegetables really help your body?" Rylan asked Mom. "Yes they do," Mom replied. "How?" asked Rylan.

"Well, broccoli helps promote strong bones and helps you heal quickly when you get cuts or scraps. Cabbage helps your bones and your brain too," Mom answered.

"And what about tomatoes?" Rylan asked.

"Tomatoes help prevent diseases like cancer. But because of its seeds, a tomato is actually a fruit," Mom informed, kissing Rylan's forehead before returning downstairs.

After Mom left out of the room, Rylan thought about all the reasons she said you should eat vegetables.
Rylan decided he should probably give them a try. But, when Skylar told him that dinner was ready, he claimed that he had a tummy ache and needed to skip dinner.

The next day at school, Rylan gobbled down the lasagna and the mashed potatoes.

Then he ate the three apple slices.

"Thought you didn't eat vegetables?" Natalie voiced.

Rylan had forgotten that potatoes were vegetables. They weren't green, and they didn't look like a flower or plant.

"Leave me alone!" Rylan responded.

Walking home from school, Rylan asked Abigail, "How do your vegetables really taste after you pour ketchup on them?" "They taste good with ketchup. But not so good without ketchup," Abigail answered. Rylan thought that maybe he should use some type of sauce to cover his vegetables too.

That night, Daddy picked up dinner from the Gobble-Gobble House. "No vegetables, no red velvet cake," Dad said. Both Rylan and Abigail feared that they would not be allowed to sink their teeth into the deliciously moist red velvet cake.

Dad, Mom and Skylar quickly dug into their meals. Abigail hesitated before taking a bite of anything, because there was no ketchup.

"The slaw is like sandwich spread," Skylar told Abigail. "You like sandwich spread on your bologna."

Abigail tried the slaw and liked it. She decided to use the slaw as a dip to eat her corn and celery.

Dad suggested to Abigail, "Why don't you use the ranch dressing. It's in the condiment bag." "No thank you," Abigail replied, continuing to use the slaw as dip. Rylan finally began eating, starting with his wings.

Everyone had finished eating dinner and were eating red velvet cake, except for Rylan. Rylan really wanted cake, but he hated the thought of those yucky vegetables going into his mouth. If only he could eat them without tasting them. If only he was like his little sister. Then he thought of what he'd do. "May I have two packets of ranch, please?" Rylan asked Dad.

Rylan was still a little hesitant to eat his vegetables, even though he really wanted cake. But then he thought about his conversation with Mom and all the important reasons to eat vegetables.

So, Rylan began dipping vegetables into the ranch dressing and eating them. Before he knew it, his corn and celery were gone.

"All you have left is your slaw," Mom said proudly.

Rylan took a deep breath and ate all of his slaw until it was gone. "I'm proud of you, Son," His dad said, handing Rylan the last slice of red velvet cake. After that day, Rylan tried his vegetables every day at school and at home for dinner.

Rylan's new motto became, "I will always try my vegetables no matter what."

THINKING QUESTIONS

	Why do you think that Rylan doesn't like vegetables?
	How do you think the ketchup makes Abigail's vegetables taste?
	Why do you think Rylan gets upset when Natalie tells him that the potatoes, he ate were vegetables?

RECALLING THE EVENTS

	Why does Rylan get sent to his room during dinner?
	How many times does Rylan mistakenly eat vegetables during this story?
	How does mom convince Abigail to eat her broccoli?
	What close family member comes to Rylan's mind when he and Mom discuss the benefits of eating vegetables?

MORE ABOUT THE STORY

	What is the name of this book?
	Who are the Authors of this book?
	Who are the Illustrators of this book?
	Who are the main characters in this story?
	What is the mood of the main character? Why does he/she feel this way?
	Does the main character resolve his/ her problem in the end? If so, how is the problem resolved?
	What does the Author want children to learn when they read or hear this story?

VEGETABLE OR FRUIT?

✓ Vegetables are leaves, flowers, roots, stems and other parts of a plant that are used as food except for the parts that have seeds.

✓ Fruits are any edible part of a plant that holds seed.

VEGETABLES	FRUIT
Broccoli	Tomatoes
Carrots	Cucumbers
Celery	Squash
Potatoes	Pumpkin

DRAW YOURSELF EATING YOUR FAVORITE VEGETABLE

FOLLOW THE AUTHOR.

amazon

f

g

baobabpublishing.com

Characters Like Me

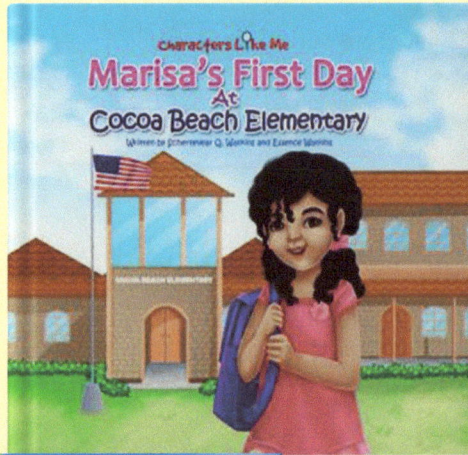

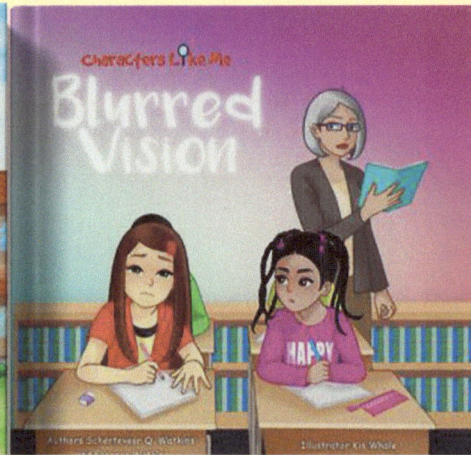

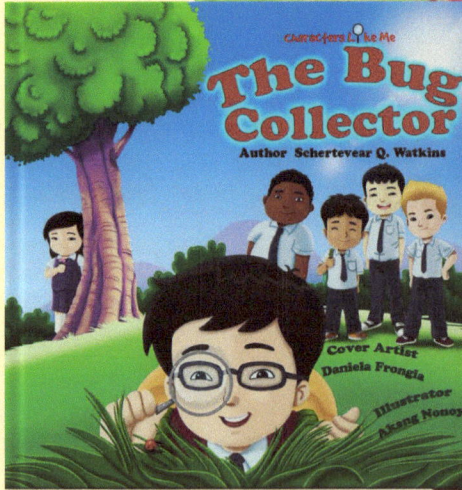

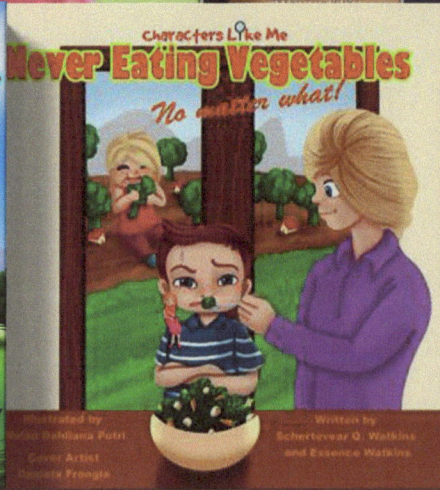

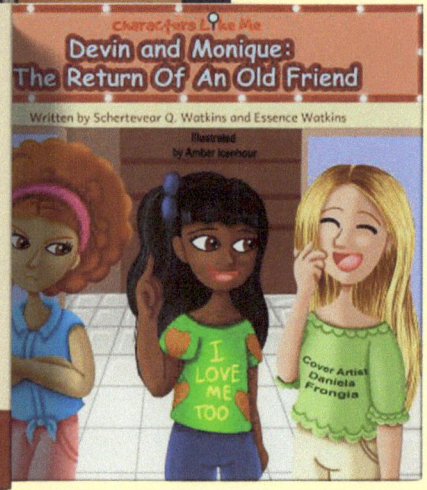

Marisa's First Day At Cocoa Beach Elementary
Written by Schertevear Q. Watkins and Essence Watkins

Blurred Vision
Authors Schertevear Q. Watkins   Illustrator Kis Whale

The Bug Collector
Author Schertevear Q. Watkins
Cover Artist Daniela Frongia
Illustrator Akang Nonoy

Never Eating Vegetables
No matter what!
Illustrated by Bella Baldiana Petri
Cover Artist Daniela Frongia
Written by Schertevear Q. Watkins and Essence Watkins

Devin and Monique: The Return Of An Old Friend
Written by Schertevear Q. Watkins and Essence Watkins
Illustrated by Amber Icenhour
Cover Artist Daniela Frongia

baobabpublishing.com

DON'T FORGET TO REVIEW THIS BOOK

Scan Here

amazon

www.ingramcontent.com/pod-product-compliance
Lightning Source LLC
LaVergne TN
LVHW072057070426
835508LV00002B/138